DRAWINGS
Degas

DRAWINGS

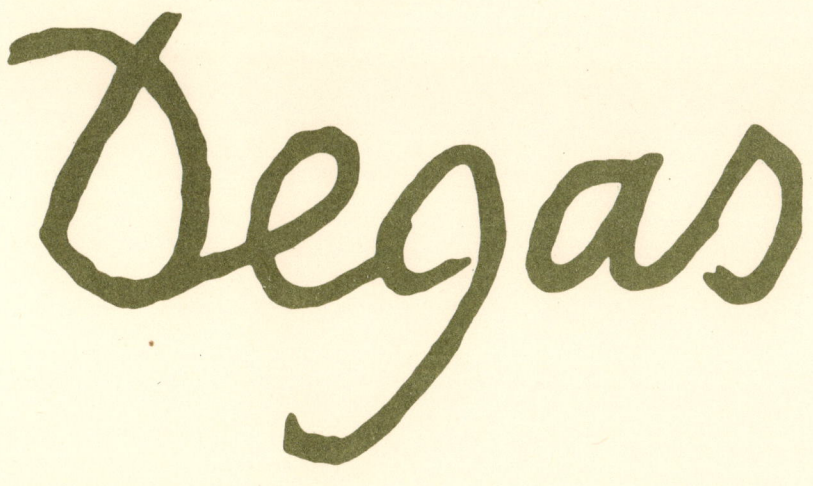

BY RONALD PICKVANCE
AND JAROMÍR PEČÍRKA

PAUL HAMLYN
LONDON · NEW YORK · SYDNEY · TORONTO

New edition rewritten by Ronald Pickvance
Selection of illustrations by Jaromír Pečírka
Graphic design by Zdeněk Sklenář

Designed and produced by Artia for
THE HAMLYN PUBLISHING GROUP LTD
LONDON · NEW YORK · SYDNEY · TORONTO
Hamlyn House, Feltham, Middlesex, England

© 1963 by Artia
Illustrations © 1963 by S. P. A. D. E. M., Paris
Second edition 1969

Printed in Czechoslovakia by Polygrafia, Prague
S 2292

CONTENTS

I. DEGAS'S LIFE 7

II. DEGAS'S DRAWINGS 10

NOTES ON THE TEXT 20

NOTES ON THE PLATES 21

BIBLIOGRAPHY 29

PLATES 31

I. DEGAS'S LIFE

Degas's life does not conform to the popular image of the nineteenth-century artist. It contains no myths of Bohemian privation, flamboyant anti-establishment poses, revolutionary intent, or squalid personal scandals—at least two of which are necessary for popular acclamation. But one myth does surround him: that of a cantankerous, secretive, sharp-tongued misogynist. The myth was self-created; it served as a carapace against intrusions on the well-ordered privacy of his one love—his work. Degas sought no public image; neither honours, like Manet, nor notoriety, like Whistler. He once said that he wished to be famous, but unknown. Any account of his life, then, must largely centre round his work.

Hilaire Germain Edgar Degas was born in Paris on July 19, 1834, the eldest of five children. His father, Pierre-Auguste-Hyacinthe de Gas (it was thus that the family spelt their name and thus that Degas signed his work until the early 1870s), managed the Paris branch of the family bank, which had been founded by Degas's grandfather in Naples, where the latter had fled from the Revolution. His mother was of Creole origin from New Orleans. The family connections in Naples and New Orleans were to affect Degas's life and to influence his art. He stayed in Naples as a young man and was still visiting the city as late as 1906. From 1857 until at least 1880, his many Neapolitan relatives frequently sat to him for their portraits. The ties with New Orleans were further strengthened in 1869, when Degas's brother, René, married his cousin, Estelle Musson. Shortly afterwards, his second brother, Achille, also married a New Orleans woman. Both brothers joined their uncle's cotton business there, and Degas visited them in 1872—73 when he again produced a series of family portraits, the most famous of which is *The Interior of the Cotton Office*.

His mother died in 1847, by which time Degas had entered the Lycée Louis-le-Grand, where he received a sound classical education, his best subjects being Greek, Latin, History and Recitation. The literary sources of two of his history-pictures, *The Young Spartans* and *Alexander and Bucephalus*, lie in Plutarch; and in his old age Degas still read Theocritus and Virgil in the original. He passed his baccalauréat with success in 1853 and was destined for the law. But his inclinations lay elsewhere. He enrolled in the print room of the Bibliothèque Nationale, where he made copies after engravings. In 1854, he studied under Lamothe, a minor disciple of Ingres, and in April 1855 entered the Ecole des Beaux-Arts. The real scene of his apprenticeship, however, was the Louvre. He haunted the galleries there, copying from paintings by the Old Masters and from sculpture, ancient and Renaissance. Degas's experiences were extended through his father, a cultured man, more than commonly interested in music and painting, who took him to see the distinguished collections of his friends Lacaze, Marcille and Valpinçon. It was the young Degas's intervention that persuaded Valpinçon to lend Ingres's *Odalisque with a Turban* (now known as the *Valpinçon Nude*) to the large International Exhibition of 1855. Degas's life-long devotion to Ingres dates from this time.

In 1856, Degas made his first visit to Italy, staying in Naples and Rome. In Rome, his friends included Gustave Moreau, Delaunay and Bonnat, who were students at the French Academy in the Villa Medici. Degas would join them there to draw from the model in traditional studio poses. In addition, he observed local costumes for possible genre pictures, produced the occasional landscape and began studies for a composition based on Dante. But, above all, he continued his self-imposed apprenticeship, copying assiduously in museum, church and gallery. Only recently has the full extent of his copying activities been realized. He was the last great copyist in European painting. In 1858–59, he stayed with his aunt and her family in Florence. The result was his first major work, a large group portrait of the Bellelli family, which he completed on his return to Paris.

An intense admiration for the work of Delacroix showed itself in the spring of 1859. He copied Delacroix's work at the Salon and elsewhere; and the influence is apparent in the colour and composition of his first history-picture, *The Daughter of Jephthah*, of 1859–60. His admiration for Delacroix continued throughout his life; in 1893, when Delacroix's *Journal* was published, he had his maid Zoë read it to him. Clearly he saw no inconsistency in revering both Ingres and Delacroix. Other history-pictures occupied him until 1865, the last of which, *Scene of War in the Middle Ages*, was exhibited at the Salon of that year. But Degas had still to make his mark. His early self-portraits—and after 1865 he never produced another—show a withdrawn, vulnerable, somewhat imperious youth. They are honest, direct, unrhetorical, with no attempt at self-glorification, and only the remotest hints of a subdued Romanticism, traces of which may also be found in his early notebooks.

New friends and new influences gradually released him from his introspection and isolation. He met Manet, probably in 1862, and by 1865 he was frequenting the Café Guerbois, the haunt of Manet, Zola, Duranty, Fantin and the young Impressionists. He came under the influence of the recently-discovered Japanese prints and of early photography. All this affected the course of his painting. After 1865 he abandoned history-painting and found new subjects in the race course and the theatre. In 1866, he sent to the Salon *The Wounded Jockey* and in 1868, *Mlle Fiocre in the Ballet 'La Source'*. His remaining exhibits at the Salon were portraits—the last in 1870.

During the Franco-Prussian War, Degas served in an artillery unit of the Garde Nationale, where he met a former school-friend, Henri Rouart. Rouart was a successful industrialist and keen painter, and his family remained life-long friends of Degas, as well as sitters for many portraits and discriminating collectors of his work. After his brief interlude in New Orleans in the winter of 1872–73, Degas rejoined his Parisian friends, who now foregathered at the Café de la Nouvelle-Athènes. The major topic of conversation was the problem of exhibiting. Despite many setbacks, Manet and Fantin wished to continue at the Salon. The rest looked for new ways of bringing their work before the public, and Degas not only joined them but became a prominent organizer of the first Impressionist exhibition of 1874. He was to exhibit at seven of the eight Impressionist exhibitions. Unlike the major Impressionists, however, he had no real interest in landscape, no desire to paint directly from nature, and based his art firmly on drawing. But the looser, broader oil technique, the acute observation of the effects of interior light, the exploitation of new media such as *essence* and monotype (for an explanation of these see pages 14 and 15 respectively), and his mature assimilation of the influences of the Japanese print and photography, place his work squarely in the camp of the moderns. He took up themes which found parallel treatment in the naturalist novels of Goncourt, Zola and the young Huysmans: not merely jockeys and dancers, but laundresses, milliners, café-concert singers and brothel scenes.

The series of brothel interiors was done in monotype, a medium which Degas began to experiment with in the early seventies and which continued to occupy him intermittently until the early nineties. He had already done some etching in his early years (1855–65), mostly portraits; the etchings of his middle period show his new range of subject-matter. He also took up lithography, which culminated in a series of nudes about 1891. At the sixth Impressionist exhibition of 1881, he showed the sculpture, *Ballet Dancer Dressed*. He continued to sculpt—horses, dancers and nudes—until 1912. After his death, seventy-three of these were cast in bronze.

Degas's studio, his small circle of friends and the sources of his art, all lay in Paris. There, his faithful maid would look after his needs, just as Delacroix had been protected by the redoubtable Jenny le Guillou. Unlike Delacroix, Degas had no love affairs; he enjoyed the society of women, but avoided any deep attachment. He was happy to dine with the Rouarts or the Halévys—although, after the Dreyfus affair in 1898, he broke with the Halévys and with all his Jewish friends. Summers might be spent at Etretat (1882), at Ménil Hubert in Normandy with his Valpinçon friends (1884 and 1892), or at Dieppe with the Halévys (1885); or he would take cures at Cauterets (1888–90), at Mont St Doré (1897) and in the Vosges mountains (1907). In 1889 he accompanied the painter Boldini on a visit to Spain and Morocco. In the following year, he took a trip by horse and tilbury through Burgundy with his sculptor friend Bartholomé. From this journey resulted a series of monotype landscapes, done from memory, and many heightened with pastel, which were exhibited at the Durand-Ruel gallery in 1892. Otherwise, he ceased to exhibit and allowed only a fraction of his work to go to his dealers, Durand-Ruel, Vollard and Bernheim-Jeune.

His late style was announced at the last Impressionist exhibition of 1886, where he showed a 'series of female nudes, bathing, washing, drying, rubbing down, combing their hair or having it combed'. Although he still produced dance and horse pictures, as well as several portraits, his late work was dominated by the series of women at their toilet. Pastel became his favourite medium; by means of a fixative which he evolved with the help of an Italian painter, Chaliava, the secret of which appears to have died with them, he was able to build up his pastels in superimposed hatchings and layers, virtually in the manner of oil-painting. On the few occasions that he did paint, the handling became extremely broad (often he would use his thumb) and the treatment simplified.

Other interests marked his later years. In the 1880s, encouraged by Heredia and Mallarmé, he tried his hand at poetry; several sonnets survive, on subjects already familiar—the dance and the horse. He also became an enthusiastic photographer, arranging his friends in groups which sometimes echo the composition of his paintings. His interest in photography and his desire for accurate depiction of pose and gesture led him to make use of Muybridge's discoveries on the movements of the horse. This is apparent in several drawings, pastels and sculptures. Above all, his last years were characterized by an intense passion for collecting. Dominated by the paintings and drawings of Ingres and Delacroix, his collection also included works by Manet, Pissarro, Renoir, Sisley, Cézanne, Gauguin and Van Gogh, as well as a fine selection of lithographs by Daumier and Gavarni.

Even in the 1870s Degas had complained about his eyesight. The threat of blindness hung over his old age, his last letters speak of his fear and frustration, yet he continued to work. The final blow came in 1912, when he was forced to move from his studio in the rue Victor Massé. He never bothered to arrange his possessions in his new studio on the Boulevard Clichy and he ceased working. But he could still be seen walking unaided around Paris, a tragic, even heroic figure, who has been compared to Homer and King Lear. He died on September 27, 1917, aged eighty-three, and was buried in the family vault in Montmartre. He once told Forain that he wanted no funeral oration. 'If there has to be one, you, Forain, get up and say, "He greatly loved drawing. So do I." And then go home.'

II. DEGAS'S DRAWINGS

'Yesterday I saw at Joyant's an album of reproductions of drawings by Degas, produced by Manzi. It was staggering; it is there that one sees that Degas is truly a master. It is more beautiful than Ingres, and, damn it, it is modern.'[1] Camille Pissarro's words, from a letter of January 1898, contain in embryo three aspects of Degas's drawing which have most occupied the attentions of later commentators. First, that in his drawings 'one sees that Degas is truly a master'; secondly, that they are 'more beautiful than Ingres'; and finally, that they are 'modern'. These three concepts are worth considering for a moment from Pissarro's point of view.

The notion that the real test of an artist's worth lies in his drawings, that there may be found the basis of his mastery, has a curiously traditional ring. Such an idea is anathema to the Impressionist concept of working directly from nature and discarding the use of preliminary drawings. Equally surprising, coming from an Impressionist, is the implication that Ingres provides the norm or touchstone when one speaks of nineteenth-century drawing. But the spectre of Ingres had substance. Several artists felt the need of the discipline which he seemed to personify. In 1867, Whistler, writing to Fantin-Latour, regretted that he had not studied under Ingres; in the early 1880s Renoir rejected his facile painterly style and went back to a self-imposed course in drawing, based largely on Ingres's example; and even Pissarro himself made a copy of Ingres portrait, *La Belle Zélie*, at Rouen in 1895. Whistler might wish for Ingres and Renoir try to emulate him; but for Pissarro, Degas surpasses Ingres, the accepted canon of 'beautiful' drawing.

Pissarro sees Degas's drawings as 'modern', a concept which had preoccupied the more progressive painters and critics ever since Baudelaire's famous *Salon of 1845*. Through Courbet and Duranty, Manet and Zola, the Impressionists and Huysmans, the idea had been tossed about and endlessly debated. For Pissarro, as for the rest of them, it meant essentially a choice of subject from the contemporary scene, rather than the perpetuation of archaizing subjects drawn from myth, bible and history. But it also implied, as Duranty had written, a means of realizing the chosen subject in a style that was the artist's own and owed nothing to the mannerisms of the Old Masters.

Pissarro's enthusiastic comments were sparked off by the publication of the *Album Manzi*. This consisted of twenty drawings, covering the years from 1861 to 1896. It was probably Manzi's expertise in the task of reproduction that persuaded Degas to agree to the album at a time when he had apparently withdrawn from the everyday world of exhibitions and publicity. It began with early studies of the nude and of draped figures which Degas had drawn for his history pictures. It continued with jockeys, portraits and dancers of the 1860s and 1870s, and concluded with various dancers of the 1880s and two nudes of 1896. It thus formed a miniature retrospective and was the first attempt to show something of Degas's achievement as a draughtsman. Previously, only a handful of drawings had been exhibited—at the second Impressionist exhibition of 1876, for example—and the occasional one had been reproduced (*e.g.* plate 38 in *La Vie Moderne* of 1879). Degas preferred to hoard them in his portfolios, so that even his most intimate friends could have no conception of their number. Some twenty of his late charcoal drawings were acquired by his dealer Vollard, who included them in an album of ninety-eight works by Degas, published in 1914 (plates 54, 55, 63, 64). But it was not until after Degas's death in 1917 that the extent of his activity as a draughtsman was fully revealed. The catalogues of the four studio sales of 1918–19 illustrated more than 1,400 drawings: a vast quantity, the existence of which Pissarro could hardly have suspected twenty years earlier.

Degas's life-work began humbly enough in 1853 when he registered in the print room of the Bibliothèque Nationale. There, he made drawings, often indeed tracings, of engravings by Marcantonio Raimondi or after Poussin. It continued, briefly, at the Ecole des Beaux-Arts and, more significantly, in the Louvre and in Italy (1856–60). He made many tentative copies from casts of the Parthenon frieze, with nothing of the brio or bold generalizations of the young Géricault or Delacroix. By comparison, his early work was cautious, somewhat uninspired and unrebellious. But his range of interests spread far beyond that of the more tepid followers of Ingres. This may be seen in the five hundred or so copies, drawn and painted, which he made after earlier masters.[2] In addition to Poussin, Raphael, Michelangelo, Leonardo and the Quattrocento (especially Mantegna), he copied Clouet, Holbein, Bronzino, Dürer, Rembrandt, Velasquez, Bellini, Titian, Veronese, Sebastiano del Piombo, Rubens, Van Dyck, Lawrence, Delacroix and Ingres. He extended his horizons to Egyptian and Persian sources, admired the *Pietà d'Avignon*, and enthused over the church of Assisi. Through his copies alone, he created his own imaginary museum. And perhaps because of this he never felt impelled, like Reynolds or Lawrence, or his own contemporary and early friend, Léon Bonnat, to form a collection of Old Master drawings. More strange is the rarity with which specific poses and compositional devices from earlier masters reappear in his own work. Unlike Manet, he did not plagiarize the Old Masters.

His first independent drawings—studies from studio models and portraits of himself, his friends or his family—already have a touch of sharp observation and a quiet strength which immediately raise them above the derivative, spineless productions of a typical Ingres follower. He does not strive for a monumentality that is beyond him; his rephrasing of Ingres is more in the key of the Quattrocento than of Raphael or Poussin. His early costume study (plate 1), drawn during his stay in Rome in 1856, shows an interest in the surface of the drapery rather than in fully expressing the volume of the figure. The style is dry and deliberate, but the pose contains in the spread of the foreshortened fingers hints of future ambitions.

Degas prepared himself slowly. He was bowled over by Delacroix at the Salon of 1859, but he steered clear of adulation. If, in his five history-pictures (1860–65), his colour is Delacroix chastened, his drawing is Ingres 'naturalized'. His increasing assurance may be seen in the preparatory studies for these history-pictures. He followed the traditional academic formulae: studies from the nude model, costume studies, compositional studies and a final working drawing. The study of a nude for his Salon picture of 1865 (plate 5) shows how Degas relied much more than Ingres on his *tête-à-tête* with the model. He is more willing to accept the evidence of his observation, even if this makes for occasional weakness — *e.g.* the right leg is unhappily realized, despite the additional strip of paper at the bottom. Degas's line does not spring free from the model, like Delacroix's more impetuous calligraphy; nor does it have the cold — the passionately cold — contour of Ingres, which only feeds on the model enough to obtain the desired rhythms of arabesque and pattern. Degas's nude has none of the anatomical distortions which Baudelaire saw in Ingres: 'A navel which has strayed in the direction of the ribs, or a breast which points too much towards the armpit.'[3]

Indeed, at no stage of his career did Degas slavishly follow Ingres. It was the spirit ('Draw lines, and more lines' was the master's injunction to the young Degas in 1855), the moral value ('Drawing is the probity of art'), and the example (he owned thirty-three drawings by Ingres) that guided him throughout. In the late 1880s the acquisition of a drawing of a female hand by Ingres prompted Degas to say: 'Look at those finger-nails, see how they are indicated. That's my idea of genius, a man who finds a hand so lovely, so wonderful, so difficult to render, that he will shut himself up all his life, content to do nothing else but indicate finger-nails.'[4]

Finger-nails, however, are hardly noticeable in Degas's portrait-study of Mme Hertel of 1865 (plate 7). The foreshortened hand, with the thumb casually resting beneath the chin, provides the keynote of the drawing. Rather than apply Ingres's artificial stylistic criteria—tapering a finger, fattening or elongating an arm as the case may be—Degas chooses to emphasize the natural. He skilfully heightens the informality of the pose by the slight inclination of the head, the loose strands of hair and the unconventional sideways glance. The result is a tender and intimate characterization. This was partly due to Degas's own attitude to portraiture. He never undertook commissions, but chose his own sitters from among his family and friends.

Degas's move toward an increased naturalism and a looser, more expressive manner of drawing may be followed in the later 1860s. This was in part prompted by a new group of friends which included Manet, Fantin, Duranty, Zola and the young Impressionists. Significantly, he abandoned history-pictures after 1865 and turned his attentions to contemporary subject matter, to the theatre and the race-course. With the changes in content went changes in style. The influence of photography and the recently discovered Japanese prints began to make themselves felt. These new influences may be seen in two male portraits. In that of Manet (plate 8), seated across a chair in a relaxed almost snapshot pose, he vividly captures something of the *flâneur* and dandy. But there are subtle contrasts of the rectilinear and the gently curving; and a soft light plays across the figure, which prompts Degas to note, '*l'oreille très claire*'. A certain irony lies behind this drawing. Manet is said to have first met Degas in the Louvre as the latter stood before Velasquez's portrait of the Infanta Isabella, etching directly onto the copperplate. Manet approached him with the words: 'You're quite daring to etch this way without a preliminary drawing. I would never dare to do as much!' Later, when Degas decided to make an etching of Manet—indeed, three such etchings exist—he took the precaution of first making preparatory drawings.

His study of another painter-friend, Tissot (plate 3), served as a first idea for a large portrait which is now in the Metropolitan Museum, New York. The viewpoint is slightly from above and, compared with the drawing of Manet, the disposition of the body is more open and at the same time more flattened. The new element of simplification becomes almost geometrical in the play of interconnected angles, often sharp and abrupt, relieved only by the bulb-shaped head, the top hat and the gentle S shape of the falling coat. The way in which Tissot is draped across the chair provides some insight into his character.

A different purpose lies behind Degas's portrait-study of *Mme Camus at the Piano* (plate 13). He is concerned with the effects of artificial and reflected light on the figure of his sitter. Details are simplified and the body becomes a silhouette. This more tonal drawing, executed in charcoal, hints at the broader style to come. Other studies for the portrait (which was refused at the Salon of 1869) were worked in pastel, and also show Degas's greater concern for a more 'painterly' drawing.

Mme Camus belonged to a circle of music-lovers which included Degas's father, the Manets and the Morisots. Several of Degas's pictures reflect this musical milieu. He portrayed his friend, Desiré Dihau, playing the bassoon in the orchestra at the Opéra. What one imagines to be the best likeness of his father is contained in two paintings of him listening to the Spanish guitarist, Pagans: and contemporaries agreed that he captured the essence of Manet in a painting which shows him sprawled across a couch, listening to his wife playing the piano. In these paintings the mood is quiet and contemplative. But in *The Song*, for which two studies exist (plates 14, 15), he creates a more animated composition. There are clearly dramatic intentions here—in a curious way, it takes on the aspect of a modern Annunciation. The drama may also be seen in the manner of drawing, rapid, lively and abrupt; in plate 14, a multi-directional shower of strokes aptly suggests the moving figure.

The subject-picture element in *The Song*, with its inherently dramatic situation, might find echoes in a Goncourt or Zola novel. A more certain connection with the Naturalist novel is apparent in a painting now known as *The Rape*, in which a half-dressed woman is watched by a man leaning against the door of her room. Here, it would seem that Degas is illustrating a scene from Zola's novel, *Madeleine Férat*, which was published in 1868. In the study (plate 26) of a half-dressed woman—a variation in pose, oddly enough, of one of the drawings for *The Song* (plate 14)—he presents an early idea for the composition. This sketch, which is executed in oil on paper, is conceived in terms of tonal mass, rather than linear units.

Throughout the 1860s, pencil remained Degas's favourite medium. It suited him while he continued to think essentially in terms of linear organization. But once he wished to render surface textures; once he began to take more note of the effects of light; once he began to conceive his forms more in terms of mass, then pencil could no longer suffice. In its stead, charcoal, already used with effect in his study of Mme Camus, together with chalk and pastel became his chosen media. One other medium must also be mentioned: *peinture à l'essence*. *Essence* (refined turpentine) is used with ordinary oil paints from which the oil and stickiness have been removed by drying. It is a thin, quickly drying medium, which therefore demands rapid working. Its expressive possibilities may be seen in three drawings (plates 9, 10, 25).

In the *Women at the Race-course* (plate 10), the sheet has certain Old Master qualities in the repetition of studies, some twelve in all. They are seemingly haphazard, as they echo and overlap each other, yet Degas instinctively organizes their disposition, the resultant pattern being punctuated at the four corners by areas of parallel shading. There is nothing of the fashion-plate; nothing chic in the presentation. The directness of the vision shows something of Degas's high regard for the drawings of Charles Keene. From this miniature pattern-book of poses, Degas created the fashionable spectators in the enclosure at Longchamp, as they appear in two paintings. Equally the elegant gentleman with cigar and umbrella (plate 25) served as a preliminary idea (later discarded) for yet another painting of a race-course, this time in Normandy, on which Degas was engaged in 1867–68. In the manner in which pose and gesture reveal the sitter's characteristics, it is comparable to the portrait-studies of Manet and Tissot (plates 3, 8).

Degas's interest in the race-course began about 1861. At the Salon of 1866, he exhibited a large painting, *The Wounded Jockey*, a not entirely successful attempt to give monumentality to a theme long familiar in English sporting prints, the steeplechase. In the same year, he executed a group of *essence* drawings of jockeys, relentlessly investigating their many positions in the saddle, viewed from a variety of angles.[5] They then provided material for a series of paintings; for Degas's practice continued to be based on working from previously drawn studies. All his race-course pictures were composed in the studio. Moreover, none of them has any documentary value; unlike the majority of English sporting prints, none of them commemorates an actual event. Degas never recorded a particular race: he had no desire to note accurately owner's colours, nor the presence of notable horses of the day. His pictures are generalized, anonymous evocations of the race-course. What interested him was the challenge of observing the rider on horseback, rather than a jockey on a known mount. Thus, when he records a groom reining in a horse (plate 9), he concentrates on the resulting bodily tensions. The tension becomes a compositional one with the inclusion of a second study of a groom accentuating the asymmetrical layout. It is as if he had activated one of his early drawings after the Parthenon frieze.

This intensive observation of riders on horseback may also be found in a large number of pencil studies, dating from the late 1860s. The young jockey with striped sleeves (plate 11) belongs to this group. As in many of these drawings, there is a slight portrait quality, in that Degas conveys something of the specific physiognomy of the sitter. But such a consideration is incidental to the total disposition of the body. With a line that is exploratory and lively, yet ultimately firm and decisive, Degas creates a fine balance of contrasting axes.

In a letter of February 1873 to his friend Tissot, Degas wrote: 'The naturalist movement will draw in a manner worthy of the great schools and then its strength will be recognized.' This strikes a note of determined intention; it has something of a challenge and a manifesto. It implies a presentation that has nothing of the sentimental and anecdotal, but rather a sort of Zolaesque 'scientific' accuracy in the notation of pose, gesture and situation. And these are the features that characterize Degas's work of the 1870s, including his innumerable drawings of ballet-dancers. If one omits a group of early pencil studies of 1872–73, none of which are illustrated in the present volume, the drawings of dancers dating from the 1870s may be conveniently divided into two groups: those executed in chalk and charcoal, and those in *essence*. Both groups share stylistic features which relate them to Degas's current preoccupations as a painter. One finds a similar interest in mass, rather than in contour; a broad, loose treatment, in which the touches become more expressive and economical; and a definite concern with registering closely the effects of light—either the artificial light of a theatre interior, or light distilled through the windows of a rehearsal room, which in turn leads to the exploitation of *contre-jour* effects.

At first sight, many of the chalk and charcoal studies have a decorative, soufflé quality. The occasional use of pink and other coloured papers seems especially beguiling; the highlights with white might be read as deftly placed decorative accents. But to see them as objects of charm, as rephrased neo-Watteau exercises, is to misunderstand their origin and purpose. Their origin was simple: they were drawings from the model, and as such continued Degas's tireless investigation of the human form. Their purpose was equally clear: to serve as studies for paintings. And their style is suitably adjusted to the needs of the projected painting. In 1873, for example, Degas was engaged on a picture showing a rehearsal on the stage of the Opéra. Six separate studies for this painting survive, two of which are reproduced here (plates 17, 19). The strong contrasts of light and shadow are only explicable in the context of the figures' ultimate place in the painting. So accurate were Degas's predetermined intentions that each figure assumed the identical pose, attitude and lighting in the finished picture. In his concern with light, however, Degas uses it to emphasize contours and reveal form, rather than dissolve them as Impressionist light would do.

At much the same time, Degas produced two paintings showing a rehearsal taking place in a room with high windows. Two studies for these are reproduced in the present volume (plates 22, 27). Light is more diffused, less harsh, less full of contrasts than in the theatre interior. Therefore the treatment differs; the style of the drawing takes note of the different circumstances. Degas reminds himself in an inscription that 'the edge of the light is thin', and this he registers with slight touches of white on the figure of the dancer (plate 27). On the other sheet, he notes the effect of shape; he wishes 'to draw well the curve and the stages of the edge of the skirts to accentuate the movement.' And it is noticeable in both these drawings how Degas is willing to create geometrical simplifications: arcs in the upper part of the torso in plate 27, triangles in that of the other.

These, then, were working drawings, kept in portfolios and never considered as collector's pieces. Degas did not even use them as 'presentation drawings' for his friends. But the other group of dancers of the 1870s—those executed in *essence*—were treated as independent works which Degas was willing to exhibit and part with. In genesis and function, they differ from the chalk and charcoal drawings. Almost without exception, they were done in the studio from previous studies, and not in the rehearsal rooms from the model (see plates 16, 18, 20, 28 and 36, for which, in each instance, these previous drawings still exist). Their function was not to serve as preparatory studies for paintings. Degas's method of working partly accounts for their simplified expressiveness; but this is also due to the nature of the medium—volatile and quick drying, demanding a swift sureness of hand. The trails of the brush, its marks, stabs, and variations of pressure emphasize the painterly quality. This release from restricted linear effects may also be found in the monotypes which Degas began to experiment with about 1873. In these, Degas would draw rapidly with a brush on a copperplate previously covered with printers' ink and create the highlights by removing the ink with a rag or thinning it with *essence*. From this he took an impression on paper. Occasionally a much weaker second impression would be reworked with pastel. This was another example of Degas's flair for experiment with new technical procedures.

When Degas exhibited several of his *essence* drawings at the second Impressionist exhibition of 1876, Huysmans wrote thus: 'Two drawings on pink paper, in which a ballerina seen from the back and another who is tying her shoe, are realized with uncommon suppleness and vigour.'[6]

One of these is clearly plate 34 in the present volume; the other is now in the Cabinet des Dessins at the Louvre (it once belonged to the Impressionist painter, Armand Guillaumin). Another painter friend, Henri Lerolle, acquired the *essence* drawing of the yawning dancer (plate 18) in 1878. And yet another of the series (plate 20) also left Degas's studio. One may note in this latter study the piquant asymmetry of the *mise-en-page*, and emphasize again that the use of white is not to create decorative accents or abstract patterns, but to register the fall of light. But the undoubted masterpiece of this series is the drawing of the ballet master, Perrot (plate 28). During Degas's lifetime this had acquired a legendary fame; the English painter, A. S. Hartrick, tells how Paul Renouard, a now forgotten illustrator, particularly of dancers at the Opéra, referred to it as 'the most wonderful painting ever done by the master'.[7] Like the rest of them, it was based on a previous drawing which carries careful observations of light and colour: '*reflets rouge farde /rouge dans le cou/ pantalon bleu flanelle /tête rose/*'. These observations are noted less literally in the drawing than in the figure of Perrot as he appears in the painting of a rehearsal, now in the Louvre.

But Degas's work of the 1870s was not just confined to dancers (although the persistent myth that sees him as quintessentially the painter of the dance might lead one to think so). He extended his subject matter to laundresses, café-concert singers (plates 45, 46) and a circus acrobat (plate 39). And in the drawings for these we find a common characteristic: an acute awareness of the mechanics of the human body. He observes the tensions, even the contortions, resulting from a momentary action; he opts for the expressive gesture, so that, for example, we are hardly aware of the missing left arm in plate 45. Yet all this is based on selection, not instanteity. If he overstresses the body, it is not for the sake of satire or caricature, as it might be with Lautrec. He exploits the expressive possibilities of a pose; he bends and stretches, but never dislocates the human form. For all these drawings convince by their tangible grasp of form, which raises them above the merely momentary and descriptive.

Something of the ideas and intentions that lay behind these drawings may be gathered from a passage in Edmond Duranty's *La Nouvelle Peinture*. This was a pamphlet which appeared in 1876 on the occasion of the second Impressionist exhibition. Much of what Duranty wrote echoed Degas's own ideas. 'We now no longer strive to attain calligraphy of line or contour, nor a decorative elegance of lines, nor an imitation of Greek figures of the Renaissance... Drawing, in its modern ambitions, wishes to acquaint itself with Nature so thoroughly, to embrace her so strongly, that it becomes faultless in all the relationships of forms, and knows the inexhaustible diversity of types. Let us forget the human body treated like a vase, from the aspect of its decorative roundness; let us forget the uniform monotony of the frame of the body, its muscles bulging under the skin; what we need is a distinctive note of modern man, in his own dress, in the midst of his social habits, at home or in the street... We do not want to see lines measured with compasses but forms that are alive and bold; forms that have logically developed from within.'

With Duranty's words in mind, one can examine two aspects of Degas's work in 1879, a project for sculpture and a decorative scheme. The first is credible in an artist who, however modern in choice of subject, never lost his classical sense of form. Yet when it comes to sculpture, he clearly has difficulty in conceiving in three-dimensional terms. In order to do this, he made a whole series of drawings, in which on the same sheet he presented a wide variety of view points of the model seen in the same position (plates 41, 42). It is difficult to think of a precedent for this procedure in European art. This obsession with the working out of one pose seen from many angles (but not necessarily conceived with a piece of sculpture in mind) marked much of Degas's late work.

More unexpected in the context of Degas's *oeuvre* is his pastel drawing of 1879 '*Portraits en frise pour décoration dans un appartement*', exhibited at the fourth Impressionist exhibition. Such a scheme of decoration may seem foreign to Degas's instincts and capabilities. Yet we learn from a jotting in one of his notebooks that he had in mind two compositions, possibly for a dining-room, one of a family in town, the other in the country. The project, however, was never realized. In the drawing (plate 30), it is interesting to see how he accentuates the silhouettes of the three women—by the vertical line which defines one side of the seated central figure, and by the series of near-parallel lines in the figure on the left. Once again Degas adapts his drawing technique to the needs of the moment. And the three figures almost become Quattrocento saints in modern dress, with parasol, book and hat as their distinctive emblems.

Throughout the 1870s, Degas extended his choice of subject and his means of expression. He found admirers and spokesmen in Goncourt, Huysmans and Duranty; he exhibited with the Impressionists and was particularly friendly with Pissarro and Mary Cassatt. It was she who sat in 1882 for the study of the woman adjusting her bonnet (plate 47), where again the momentary action is given a firm *disegno*—note how the arms act as compositional struts to the head. But by the early 1880s, Duranty and Manet had died; the Impressionists were breaking up, each searching for new ways of pursuing his artistic ideals. Renoir sought his way out through Ingres and the experience of Italy; Pissarro eventually threw in his lot with the young Seurat; even Monet had his moments of doubt. Of them all, Degas would seem to have the necessary background and sufficient artistic reserves to overcome any sense of crisis. Yet even he had serious misgivings. He once said: 'Everyone has talent at twenty-five—the difficult thing is to have it at fifty.' And in a letter to his friend Lerolle of August 1884, he wrote: 'If you were single, fifty years of age (for the last month) you would know similar moments when a door shuts inside one and not only on one's friends... I have made too many plans, here I am blocked, impotent. And then I have lost the thread of things. I thought there would always be enough time... I stored up all my plans in a cupboard and always carried the key on me. I have lost that key.' And to another friend, the sculptor Bartholomé, he wrote at the same time: 'Where are the times when I thought myself strong. When I was full of logic, full of plans. I am sliding rapidly down the slope and rolling I know not where, wrapped in many bad pastels, as if they were packing paper.'[8]

But Degas found his release. One subject which he had virtually ignored since his last history-picture of 1865 was the female nude. He returned to it in 1877 when he began producing a series of nudes in the monotype medium. These show three significant developments in treatment. First, the full-blooded reclining nude, harking back to certain works of Courbet of the mid 1860s; some of these served as presentation drawings for his friends. Secondly, a group of brothel interiors *(maisons closes)* which Degas reserved for his portfolios—not that they contained the least hint of pornographic intent. And, finally, a series of women at their toilet; it was these that held the key to Degas's late style.

His first dated pastels of nudes are of 1884. Two years later, he exhibited ten pastels at the last Impressionist exhibition. From then on, the nude increasingly claimed his attention. He observed the model in the simple repetition of such physical activities as bathing, washing, drying, combing her hair or having it combed. Large-scale, many figured compositions no longer interested him. The only exception is a number of pastels of bathers set in a landscape, of which plate 61 is one example. Here, he provided but a summary indication of the landscape, concentrating on the disposition of the shape and mass of the three figures. The contour has a new power and vigour. In his drawings, his sole medium was now charcoal, which provided the armature, as it were, for his many pastels (plate 57).

His *mise-en-scène* was of the simplest: frequently a bath-tub sufficed (plates 55, 57, 58). Yet he was able to evolve a range of poses and a series of inventive compositional devices which ensured the close formal relationship of model and bath. Even in a small format (plates 55 and 58), Degas can create a monumental effect. In the one, the main diagonal thrust of the body is countered by several contrasting axes. In the other, figure and bath are caught up in the same dominating rhythm. In both drawings, the contour is incisive; the modelling has no tender, systematic application—strong hatchings contrast with rubbed areas; light falls on flesh in patches and helps create the form of the figure; facial features, hands and feet are ignored—hidden in the actions of the nude, or cut off by the frame. The Louvre drawing (plate 58), and also the drawing in the Fogg Art Museum (plate 59), both illustrate a practice that Degas used increasingly in his later years: the taking of counter-proofs, simply by pressing a clean sheet of paper against an existing drawing. This enabled him to work out the possibilities of a given pose; minor readjustments would often be made to the reversed image. It sprang from his belief (expressed in a letter to Bartholomé of 1886) that: 'One must treat the same subject ten times, even a hundred times. Nothing in art should seem to be accidental, not even movement.'[9]

Another and much more prevalent way of achieving his object was his use of tracing paper. This might have begun as a mechanical aid, but it quickly became a means of subtly modifying his first intentions. Indeed, in his later works it became, as we shall see, the major support for his drawings and pastels. In 1890–91, however, he used it extensively in his attempt to capture the pose of a nude, leaning over as she dries her hip (plate 53). These many studies were used as the basis for a suite of lithographs; and eventually a piece of sculpture summed up his obsessive attachment to this particular pose. Degas thus attains an economy of statement equivalent to Cézanne's final assault on Mont Ste Victoire or Monet's late water-lilies.

The containment of shape, the balance of axes, the metope-like appropriateness of these nudes of the early 1890s gave way to a broader treatment and a more accentuated plasticity in works of the latter part of the decade. One may note the superb simplification of the back in plate 56; or the expressive surface and sculptural mass of that in plate 54. It is hardly surprising that Degas turned increasingly to sculpture. It was not merely the threat of blindness, which had haunted him since 1870; sculpture was a logical extension of his activity as a draughtsman. His sculptures realized in three dimensions what he was striving for with charcoal and pastel: a heightened sense of the human form.

It is extremely difficult to date Degas's late work. He discontinued the use of *carnets* after 1886; he ceased to exhibit after 1892; there are few clues in his letters; and while a handful of portraits and dancers are dated in the 1890s, only one nude is dated, a pastel of 1903, now in Saõ Paolo. Moreover, Degas would frequently return to the same pose after a lapse of time and produce a variation upon it; he would occasionally rework an earlier picture; and he would take up a theme which had occupied him twenty or thirty years earlier. For instance the drawing in plate 62 has precedents in both subject and style. It first appears on a sheet dating from the mid 1870s, which shows the pair from the front, from which Degas produced a finished pastel, omitting however the kneeling figure. The theme is more directly suggested in certain pastels of 1886, where the attributes of Pierrot and Colombine are clear, possibly deriving from an actual performance staged at the Opéra in January of that year. Degas then abandoned the theme, but took it up again about 1900. Now there are significant changes. The identity of Pierrot and Colombine is lost and the reference to a stage performance removed. One is not sure whether the figures are clothed or nude—the one on the left appears to be in tights but is bare-footed, while the other seems to be nude, but wears dancing slippers. In other words, all descriptive and evocative elements are banished. The presentation is abrupt, simplified and brutal. The kneeling figure's buttocks become a flattened oval, and a continuous thick line runs from the right arm-pit, down the haunches, round the right leg to the foot, four changes of plane occur *en route*. Equally, the modelling is minimal, a few arbitrary marks here and there, while light strikes in large areas, its delicate transitions no longer recorded. Yet the composition has innumerable complexities, subtle contrasts of shape and interval, implied depth yet apparent flatness. Degas repeated it in several drawings, pastels, and one small painting. In the majority of these, he shows the pair in exactly the same pose, but seen from the front. This was yet another means—with the counter-proof and the use of tracing-paper—of pushing further the implications of a given pose; and it emphasizes the sculptural vision of his late work.

In the drawing of two laundresses (plate 63) Degas returned again to a theme which he had first used in the 1870s. But now the cryptic, searing strokes of charcoal on tracing-paper and the utter lack of interest in particularization of form make this a typical late drawing. It was one of the few which Degas signed and sold to his dealer, Vollard.

We have one eye-witness account of Degas at work in his last years. Moreau-Nélaton, artist, writer and collector, visited Degas's studio in December, 1907.[10] He found him working on a pastel showing a woman leaving her bath, her maid in the background, a chair in the foreground with a salmon-pink *peignoir* thrown over it. The drawing was done on tracing-paper. Moreau-Nélaton then accompanied Degas to the shop of Lésin, who carried out the difficult operation of glueing the tracing-paper to cardboard. Degas hesitated before allowing Lésin to complete the operation. 'The maid's head touches the top edge of the drawing. If we do not take a little off the bottom the balance will be missing.' Two centimetres were cut off the bottom. This story illustrates Degas's continuing concern with the precise pictorial balance of his works. But he would find it empirically, either by adding strips of paper to the original drawing, or, as here, by removing a strip.

Moreau-Nélaton described the style of the pastel as 'somewhat summary, like everything that Degas makes now, with his eyesight daily growing feebler; what a vigorous and grandiose drawing! The hand gripping the bath, indicated by a single stroke, is admirable.' These remarks could be applied to the drawing of the nude leaving her bath, with her maid in attendance (plate 64), which must date from about 1907. The violent elisions of form and the repetitively vertical striations of charcoal give the image a monumental power.

These late charcoal drawings have often been seen as painful evidence of Degas's battle against his threatened blindness. Yet from the tragic arose the heroic—Renoir compared one to the Parthenon frieze. They supremely sum up his lifelong obsession with the human form. For we must accept the limits of Degas's interests, which excluded still-life, landscape (except as an incidental activity) and imaginative compositions; and which never entered the realms of allegory, symbolism or social comment. At no time in his career did he seek surface charm, linear arabesque or decorative elegance. These late drawings have an autonomous grandeur and an essential probity which reject sleight-of-hand, repetitive formulae and paraded virtuosity. In his own words: 'No art was ever less spontaneous than mine. What I do is the result of reflection and study of the great masters; of inspiration, spontaneity, temperament I know nothing.'

NOTES ON THE TEXT

1 Camille Pissarro. *Lettres à Son Fils Lucien*, 1950, p. 447
2 For Degas's activities as a copyist, see Professor Theodore Reff's series of articles in the *Burlington Magazine* (June 1963, June 1964, June 1965, and December 1965)
3 Charles Baudelaire. *The Mirror of Art*, edited by Jonathan Mayne, 1955, p. 205
4 George Moore. 'Degas: The Painter of Modern Life' in *The Magazine of Art*, 1890, p. 419
5 The drawings are illustrated in Lemoisne, nos. 151—162
6 J. K. Huysmans. *L'Art Moderne*, 1883, p. 127
7 A. S. Hartrick. *A Painter's Pilgrimage*, 1939, p. 87
8 *Degas Letters*, 1947, pp. 80—81
9 *Degas Letters*, 1947, p. 117
10 Etienne Moreau-Nélaton. 'Deux Heures avec Degas' in *L'Amour de l'Art*, July 1931, pp. 267—70

NOTES ON THE PLATES

The references are confined to the following: (1) The four catalogues of Degas's studio sale of 1918—19 (IV 104 means Fourth sale, lot 104); (2) Lemoisne's catalogue raisonné (1947—49); (3) H. Rivière, *Les Dessins de Degas* (1922—23); (4) Vollard's Album of 98 reproductions of Degas's work (1914). These are abbreviated to L, R, and V, respectively, followed by the relevant number. Wherever known, the present location of the drawings is given.

1 *Roman Beggar Woman*. Pencil on light green paper, 41 × 29 cm., signed: *Rome 1856*. IV 104, R I.
   Degas first visited Rome in 1856. The present drawing, with its study of drapery on the verso, is connected with a painting (L 29), which is dated 1857, as also is a related painting (L 28), now in Birmingham City Art Gallery. Other costume-studies executed in Rome exist—among them are three watercolours (L 16—18) and two drawings (IV 68 a, b).

2 *Portrait of a Seated Woman*. Pencil, 29 × 22 cm., *circa* 1860—61. III 152 i, R 53.
   The identity of the sitter is problematical. Rivière compares her with drawings of Degas's sister, Marguerite (II 240, 241, IV 89 b), which acted as studies for two paintings, now in the Louvre (L 60—61). In all these, Marguerite is seen full-face; but the central parting of the hair, the lace bonnet and the scalloped collar reappear here, and the style of the drawing suggests a similar date of 1860—61. Notice, how the setting is only summarily suggested; Degas's interest clearly lay in the head and the lace bonnet.

3 *Portrait of Tissot*. Black crayon, 31 × 35 cm., *circa* 1866. III 158 i, R 4. Fogg Art Museum, Cambridge, Mass.
   The painter J.-J. Tissot (1836—1902) was an early friend of Degas and they remained on close terms until the late 1870s. In this portrait-study, the image of the Baudelairean dandy is conveyed in the informal, relaxed pose. A related study (III 158 iii) shows differences in the position of both arms and legs; these are nearer to the final painting (Metropolitan Museum, New York; L 175) where, however, Degas further heightens his rakish appearance by adding a cane, lightly held in the right hand. Two studies of Tissot's head were made on another sheet (III 158 ii) and further studies appear in two of Degas's notebooks.

4 *Study of Two Clothed Figures*. Pencil, 32.8 × 21.5 cm., *circa* 1859—60. Part of I 6, R 58.
   Although there are no specific parallels for these two figures in the finished painting, they form part of the exploratory stages for Degas's first history picture, *The Daughter of Jephthah* (L 94), on which he was engaged in 1859—60.

5 *Standing Nude*. Pencil, 36 × 22 cm., 1865. Part of I 13, R 13. Musée du Louvre, Paris.
   One of many drawings of the female nude which served as studies for the painting *Scene of War in the Middle Ages*, exhibited at the Salon of 1865. Whatever its subject matter (and recently it has been suggested that the event depicted refers to the American Civil War and New Orleans, and not to Orléans and war in the Middle Ages), the picture formed a suitable exercise as an academy of the female nude, seen in a variety of poses.

6 *Study of an Archer*. Pencil, sanguine and white crayon on grey paper, 22.9 × 35.5 cm., 1865. Part of I 13, R 14. Musée du Louvre, Paris.

Like the previous drawing, this is a study for Degas's Salon picture of 1865. The figure was based on a nude-study—in fact, the sanguine lines apparent in the drawing were traced on the sheet from the original nude-study to form a working basis for the pose. The practice of moving from studies of the nude to the clothed model goes back to the Renaissance and is frequently found in Ingres.

7 *Portrait of Mme Hertel.* Pencil, 36×23 cm., signed and dated 1865. I 312, R 59. Fogg Art Museum, Cambridge, Mass.
None of Degas's portrait drawings were done as commissions. Unlike Ingres, therefore, he was free to concentrate on what he considered the essentials, in this case the head and its relationship to the foreshortened hand. The figure occupies the centre of the sheet; but in the related painting, Woman with Chrysanthemums (Metropolitan Museum, New York; L 125), she appears on the extreme right, seated at a table on which is placed a large bowl of flowers, an early instance of Degas's fondness for an asymmetrical composition.

8 *Portrait of Manet.* Pencil on pink paper, 41×28 cm., *circa* 1865. R 60. Mme Ernest Rouart, Paris.
One of three drawings of Edouard Manet (1832–83), which Degas presented to his friend Ernest Rouart on the occasion of his marriage to Julie Manet, daughter of Eugène Manet and Berthe Morisot. The two artists met in the early 1860s; the present sheet was used as the preparatory study for an etching of Manet seated. Three other drawings of Manet are in the Metropolitan Museum, New York (II 210).

9 *Two Studies of a Groom. Essence* and gouache on ochre paper, 25×34.2 cm., *circa* 1866. III 153 ii, R 16, L 382. Musée du Louvre, Paris.
Degas's observation of horse and jockey, either at the races or in the country, began about 1861. Many drawings are concerned with the horse alone; in others, as here, he concentrated on capturing the pose of the rider. Two related studies of grooms exist (L 383 and 383 *bis*). Compare in style and technique with plates 10 and 25.

10 *Studies of Women at the Race-course. Essence* on oiled ochre paper, 45×31 cm., *circa* 1866. III 153 i, R 65, L 259. Musée du Louvre, Paris.
Together with two other sheets (L 260 and 261), this series of studies was used for the fashionable spectators seen in the background of two race-course pictures set at Longchamp (L 258 and 262). Compare in style and technique with plates 9 and 25.

11 *Study of a Young Jockey.* Pencil, 28.5×23 cm., *circa* 1866. III 129 iii, R, 63.
This sensitive pencil study has, like several of Degas's early drawings of jockeys, a certain portrait-quality. Three other drawings show a young jockey in similarly striped colours: III 92 iii, III 107 ii, IV 274.

12 *Study of a Woman's Arm.* Charcoal and pastel, 31×23 cm., *circa* 1892. IV 262 b, R 18, L 1108.
At the Salon of 1868, Degas exhibited the painting *Mlle Fiocre in the Ballet 'La Source'* (Brooklyn Museum, New York; L 146). Shortly afterwards, in trying to remove the varnish, he ruined certain parts of the picture. In the early 1890s, he decided to restore it. The present drawing, and another study of a hand and foot (L 1109), were used as guides in the re-painting of the right foreground figure.

13 *Study for the Portrait of Mme Camus at the Piano.* Charcoal, 35×22 cm., 1869. III 152 ii, R 19.
This is a squared-up study for a portrait, now in the Bührle Collection, Zurich (L 207),

which was apparently refused at the Salon of 1869. There are also five pastel studies (L 208–12). Mme Camus was an accomplished musician. A second portrait of her, exhibited at the Salon of 1870, is now in the National Gallery of Art, Washington (L 271).

14 *Study of a Woman*. Pencil, 48×30 cm., *circa* 1869. III 404 i, R. 20. Musée du Louvre, Paris.

15 *Study of a Woman*. Pencil, 48×30 cm., *circa* 1869. III 404 ii, R 21. Musée du Louvre, Paris.
Nos. 14 and 15 are studies for the painting *The Song* (Bliss Collection, Dumbarton Oaks, Washington; L 331). On both sheets, Degas includes quick compositional sketches for the eventual picture. The sitter is said to be his sister, Marguerite (*cf.* plate 2). Taken together, the two sheets curiously resemble the traditional representation of the Annunciation.

16 *Study of Seated Dancer*. *Essence* on blue paper, 26.6×33 cm., *circa* 1873. III 132 c, R 23. Musée du Louvre, Paris.
A rapid and economical evocation of a seated dancer who reappears in the painting *Ballet Rehearsal on the Stage*, now in the Metropolitan Museum, New York (L 400). Two related studies in charcoal exist: II 333 and III 83 b.

17 *Study of Standing Dancer*. Charcoal and white chalk on faded pink paper, 45×28 cm., *circa* 1873. III 338 i, R 68.
Degas has acutely observed the effects of stage light on this dancer as she leans with her left arm against a stage-flat. It was thus that he represented her in the painting *Ballet Rehearsal on the Stage* (L 340). Several other drawings for this picture (*e.g.* I 114, II 331, II 333 and plate 19) show a similar concern with the effects of light; and in each of them, Degas' creates, with the varied pressure of his medium and its free suggestive usage, their precise appearance in the finished painting. A related pose occurs in a drawing *à l'essence* (L 401).

18 *Study of Standing Dancer, Yawning*. *Essence* on green paper, 54×45 cm., *circa* 1873. R 69, L 402. Private collection, Holland.
This rapidly brushed evocation of a yawning dancer was used, like plates 16 and 17, in the painting now in New York (L 400). Two other studies of a yawning dancer exist: II 331 and IV 276 a. The present drawing was acquired by Degas's artist-friend, Henri Lerolle, in 1878.

19 *Standing Dancer Seen from Behind*. Charcoal heightened with white on brown paper, 45×30 cm., 1873. II 327, R 70. Private collection, Paris.
This drawing, in style, technique and purpose, belongs to the same group as plate 17. Note the continued use of the plumb-line.

20 *Standing Dancer Fastening her Belt*. *Essence* on brown paper, 55×38 cm., signed lower left, *circa* 1874. R 71, L 359.
This is a pose which frequently recurs in Degas's work (*cf.* L 496, 625, 1012). But it is never so succinctly stated as here, nor with such piquant asymmetry in the *mise-en-page*. This is one of the few drawings which left Degas's studio during his lifetime.

21 *Study of Two Dancers*. *Essence* on brown paper, 30×30 cm., *circa* 1874. II 232, R 73; L 362 *bis*.
The *essence* medium again allows Degas the utmost economy. The fragmentary nature of the figure on the right is explained by her position in the final painting—she is holding on to a column. The painting (Harry Paine Bingham Collection, New York; L 362) was first exhibited in London in 1875. A related study, also in *essence*, is III 132 i.

22 *Two Studies of a Dancer*. Charcoal heightened with white on pink paper, 30×44 cm., *circa* 1874. III 359 ii, R 74. Mme E. Rouart, Paris.

These two studies are related to two paintings of the ballet class (L 399 and Wertheim Collection, Fogg Art Museum). In the long inscription Degas reminds himself 'to draw well the curve and the stages of the edge of the skirts to accentuate the movement'. A related drawing is II 346.

23 *Studies of Two Dancers*. Charcoal, white chalk and pastel on pink paper, 46×30 cm., *circa* 1876. III 209 i, R 75.
This sheet, like plate 22, is related to two separate works: the seated dancer is a study for a pastel (Metropolitan Museum, New York; L 542); and the superbly observed head reappears in a painting, now in the Paul Mellon Collection (L 625).

24 *Study of Dancer Scratching her Back*. Charcoal heightened with white, 45×30 cm., *circa* 1874. II 341 i, R 76. Musée du Louvre, Paris.
This pose went through three stages. First, a charcoal drawing, heightened with white (IV 271c), which in style is related to plates 17 and 19; then, a rapid study in *essence* (III 132 ii), similar in style to plate 16; and finally, this squared-up study, which was used for the dancer seated on the piano in the painting *The Dancing Class* (Louvre; L 341). Compare also the dated pastel of 1874 (L 343).

25 *Study of Standing Man*. Essence on oiled paper, 33×20 cm., *circa* 1868. II 49, R 77. L 344. John Seymour Thacher, Washington.
A study stylistically related to plates 9 and 10. Two other studies of fashionably dressed men, casually leaning on an umbrella (L 307–8), were also used as preparatory ideas for a painting of a race-course (L 184).

26 *Study of a Half-dressed Woman*. Oil-sketch on ochre paper applied to canvas, 61×50 cm., *circa* 1871. III 23, R 78, L 351. Basle Museum.
A pose which is a variant of plate 14—and, as there, with noticeable *pentimenti*. The study is connected with one of Degas's most dramatic subject-pictures, now known as *The Rape* (Henry P. McIlhenny Collection; L 348), which probably represents a scene from Zola's novel *Madeleine Férat* of 1868.

27 *Study of a Dancer*. Charcoal heightened with white, 44×30 cm., *circa* 1874. II 357, R 79.
Just as an earlier squared-up drawing (plate 24) resulted from other studies, so the present drawing is founded upon a more summary sketch (IV 265). The pose is faithfully transcribed in the painting *The Dancing Lesson* (L 399), for which plate 22 also acted as a study. The style of both drawings shows a similar concern with the effects of light, expressed here in the inscription: 'the edge of the light is thin.'

28 *The Dancer, Jules Perrot*. Essence on grey-green paper, 47.5×30 cm., signed and dated 1875. R 26, L 364. Henry P. McIlhenny, Philadelphia.
The loose, economical technique, evident in the *essence* drawings of dancers, achieves its apotheosis in this magnificent study of the ballet master, Perrot. Again, its genesis repeats the same process that we have observed in drawings of dancers; virtually all these were based on previous studies, rather than on direct drawings from the model. In this instance, the image is derived from a charcoal drawing (III 157 ii), which bears annotations regarding light and colour. Perrot reappears in two paintings of rehearsal, L 341 (Louvre) and L 397 (H. Paine Bingham Collection), and in two monotypes, one of which is heightened

with pastel (L 365). In addition there are three portraits of him: a painting (L 366), a pastel (L 367), and a drawing (III 157 iii).

29 *Study of Two Dancers*. *Essence* on pink paper, 22×27 cm., 1872. III 395, R 30, L 300 *bis*. Museum Boymans-Van Beuningen, Rotterdam.

A study for one of Degas's first dance pictures, now in the Louvre (L 298). Two related studies exist (L 299 and 300).

30 *Projects for Portraits in a Frieze*. Charcoal and pastel, 50×65 cm., 1879. R 28, L 532. Private collection, Paris.

The purpose behind this drawing, elucidated by the inscription—'*Portraits en frise pour décoration dans un appartement*'—is virtually unique in Degas's work. See page 17 for a fuller discussion. The drawing was exhibited at the fourth Impressionist exhibition of 1879. Two related works exist (L 533 and a pastel in a private collection, New York).

31 *Study of a Dancer*. Charcoal, 46×30 cm., *circa* 1874. III 339 ii, R 80.

A quick notation of a dancer (Melina Darde? *cf.* plates 37 and 38), whose pose is comparable to plate 20. Although squared-up for possible transfer, the figure does not occur in any existing pastel or painting.

32 *Woman with a Parasol*. *Essence* on canvas, 75×85 cm., *circa* 1872. II 36, R 81, L 414. Private collection, London.

Almost certainly a sketch of a woman at the races, comparable to two small paintings which undoubtedly depict such a theme—L 495 and L 920, the latter now in the Burrell Collection, the Art Gallery and Museum, Glasgow.

33 *Study of a Dancer*. Charcoal heightened with white, 34×29 cm., 1873. II 356, R 83.

A study for a dancer who appears in the right foreground of a painting, now in the Burrell Collection, Glasgow Art Gallery and Museum, (L 430), without, however, the distinctive stockings. Rapidly indicated behind her is the long-cloaked figure of the dresser, for which a separate study exists (IV 272 a).

34 *Dancer Adjusting her Ballet Slipper*. *Essence* on pink paper, 40×32 cm., *circa* 1875. II 245, R 31, L 388.

Another rapid *essence* sketch (*cf.* plates 18, 20, 21, 28), which was certainly exhibited at the second Impressionist exhibition of 1876. It was described by J. K. Huysmans in his earliest published reference to Degas: 'Two drawings on pink paper, in which a ballerina seen from the back and another, who is tying her shoe, are realized with uncommon suppleness and vigour.' (*L'Art Moderne*, p. 127). Although the drawing is signed—to the left of the bench—Degas retained it in his portfolios. The stamp of the studio sale appears at the lower left.

35 *Dancer at the Bar*. Charcoal, 30×20 cm., *circa* 1876. III 133 d, R 85. Musée du Louvre, Paris.

Several drawings of dancers practising at the bar exist. Compare this quick charcoal sketch with the *essence* drawing plate 36. The image appears to 'slip', as Degas searches for the pose, an effect which occurs more markedly in plate 43.

36 *Two Dancers at the Bar*. *Essence* on green paper, 48×63 cm., *circa* 1876. II 338, R 86, L 409. British Museum, London.

As in the majority of other drawings *à l'essence*, the figures on this sheet were derived from previous pencil or chalk drawings from the model (*cf.* plate 35 and III 83 c). The drawing, on the same green paper as the yawning dancer (plate 18), is related to one of Degas's most famous paintings, *Dancers at the Bar* (Metropolitan Museum, New York; L 408).

37 *Two Dancers Resting*. Charcoal heightened with white on grey paper, 30×46 cm., III 362, R 32.

These are clearly two studies from the same model—probably Melina Darde (*cf.* plates 31 and 38). While he is recording a pose, Degas also observes light and colour reflections: 'corsage reflété en rose à gauche. Joue très reflétée'. The dancer on the left reappears in another drawing (IV 275 a), while that on the right was developed in a pastel (L 626) and a painting (L 625).

38 *Melina Darde Seated*. Black pencil, 31×23 cm., 1878. II 230 i, R 33. Baroness Alain de Gunzburg, Paris.

The fuller annotation on this drawing is concerned with similar observations of light and colour as the briefer remarks on plate 37. It also contains the name of Melina Darde, a young dancer, who seems to have frequently posed for Degas. An almost identical, less finished drawing exists (Musée du Louvre; III 133 iii). The present drawing was reproduced, without the accompanying annotation, in *La Vie Moderne*, May 8, 1879.

39 *Miss La La*. Black chalk and pastel on coarse yellowish paper, 47×32 cm., 1879. IV 255 a, R 38. Barber Institute of Fine Arts, Birmingham University.

On several evenings in January 1879, Degas observed a negress, Miss La La, at the Cirque Fernando as she was pulled up to the roof by a rope held between her teeth. Many drawings resulted (L 523–25, IV 256 a, b, c). It was the present drawing, which formed the basis for the painting exhibited at the fourth Impressionist exhibition of 1879, and now in the National Gallery, London (L 522). A study of the circus interior (IV 255 b) is also in the Barber Institute.

40 *Portrait of Diego Martelli*. Charcoal and white chalk on brown paper, 44×31.3 cm., 1879. III 160 i, R 91. Cleveland Museum of Art.

Following his fascination for Miss La La, Degas transferred his attention to an Italian art critic and friend, Diego Martelli (1839–96). One drawing is inscribed 'chez Martelli 3 Avril 1879'. Other drawings are in the Fogg Art Museum and the National Gallery of Scotland. Two paintings resulted: National Gallery of Scotland (L 519) and National Museum, Buenos Aires (L 520).

41 *Three Studies of a Nude Dancer*. Charcoal heightened with white chalk on greyish green paper, 48×63 cm., 1879. III 369, R 35.

Degas's purpose in making three views of the same model in the same position was quite specific. He was thinking in terms of a possible sculpture and these studies were a means of helping him realize the pose in three-dimensional terms. In fact, this particular position did not materialize as a piece of sculpture, but is clearly connected with his preliminary ideas for the statue of the fourteen-year-old dancer (*cf.* plate 42).

42 *Four Studies for the Fourteen-Year-Old Dancer*. Charcoal, 48×30 cm., 1879. III 341 ii, R 36. Musée du Louvre, Paris.

Four different views of the same model: not, like Watteau, recorded and then stored away for possible use later in painting, but conceived specifically for immediate use—as a means of realizing his statue of the fourteen-year-old dancer. The inscription at the upper left is presumably an *aide-mémoire*—a model's address, perhaps. There are several related studies (III 149 a, III 277, III 386, IV 287 a and L 586 *bis* and *ter*), which demonstrate the thoroughness with which Degas prepared himself for his first figure sculpture.

43 *Seated Dancer Adjusting her Stocking*. Charcoal, 30×22 cm., *circa* 1880. III 112 iv, R 34.
One of some dozen-or-so studies of a dancer seated on a bench raising her right leg as she adjusts her stocking. Notice, how the image appears to shift as a result of the numerous *pentimenti*—an effect which gives the sheet a coincidental relationship to some of Daumier's drawings. The present pose was worked out in a painting now in the Yale University Art Gallery (L 1107).

44 *Study of a Standing Dancer*. Pastel on ochre paper, 60×45 cm., *circa* 1880–85. II 192, R 37, L 621.
The pose of this abruptly simplified silhouette—the dancer is seen *contre-jour*—occurs with minor modifications in several other works (II 176, IV 286c, L 479–81, 905, 911–12).

45 *Café-concert Singer*. Charcoal heightened with white on grey paper, 47×29 cm., *circa* 1878. III 342 ii, R 89. Musée du Louvre, Paris.
This close-up study of a café-concert singer served as a study for three pastels (L 477, 478, 478 *bis*), the last of which was exhibited at the fourth Impressionist exhibition of 1879.

46 *Two Studies of a Café-concert Singer*. Charcoal and pastel on grey paper, 52×63 cm., signed, *circa* 1879, R 90, L 504. Mrs John Wintersteen, Philadelphia.
This double-study of, presumably, the same performer is one of a group devoted to the café-concert. Compare the three pastels (L 505–7) and a drawing (III 335 i), where a similar performer is shown facing in the opposite direction.

47 *Woman Tying the Ribbon on her Hat*. Charcoal and pastel, 48×31 cm., *circa* 1882. II 360, R 40, L 694. Musée du Louvre, Paris.
The model in this study is the American painter and close friend of Degas's, Mary Cassatt (1845–1926). Compare the pastel now in the Museum of Modern Art, New York (L 693).

48 *Dancer at the Bar*. Charcoal heightened with white on greyish green paper, 46×29 cm., *circa* 1876. II 352, R 39.
A study, which corresponds with a figure in the painting now in the Clark Art Institute, Williamstown, Mass (L 820).

49 *After the Bath*. Oil-sketch on canvas, 151×215 cm., *circa* 1886. I 57, R 43, L 951. Brooklyn Museum, New York.
A large sketch in oils which is related to the pastel series of nudes at their toilet exhibited at the last Impressionist exhibition of 1886.

50 *Woman at her Toilet*. Charcoal and pastel, 62×47 cm., *circa* 1887. II 306, R 44, L 919. Private collection, Paris.
Two drawings which are related in pose to this study are III 288 and IV 159.

51 *Study of a Dancer*. Charcoal and pastel on ochre paper, 31×23 cm., *circa* 1882–5. III 87 iii, R 45.
Degas made more than one hundred studies of young dancers, largely for the purpose of observing the correct ballet positions. Frequently, the annotations on these drawings refer to a faulty position. Very few of these studies materialized as pastels or paintings.

52 *Study of Three Dancers*. Charcoal and pastel on grey paper, 45×59.5 cm., signed, *circa* 1880. R 95, L 579. Mr and Mrs Robert B. Honeyman, Jr., U.S.A.
'*Vue de dessus*'—seen from above—notes Degas on this drawing. And it was thus that they were seen in a pastel (L 577), showing a view of the stage from a box. A related study is L 578.

53 *After the Bath*. Charcoal on tracing paper, 41×28 cm., *circa* 1891. II 318, R 47.
A pose too frequently repeated, sometimes in reverse, for all the versions to be listed here. They were drawn in connection with a projected series of lithographs (only partially realized), which Degas was engaged upon in the early 1890s.

54 *Nude Combing her Hair*. Pastel, 42.5×28 cm., signed, *circa* 1900. R 96, V 33.
One of many late drawings acquired by the dealer Ambroise Vollard and included in his album of ninety-eight reproductions of Degas's work published in 1914.

55 *The Bath*. Pastel, 41×34 cm., signed, *circa* 1891. V 37, L 734. Mr and Mrs David Rosenthal, U.S.A.
Several pastels were devoted to the theme of a woman stepping in, or out, of her bath. Compare L 731–33, 1028–31, and 1309–10.

56 *After the Bath*. Charcoal, 60×48 cm., *circa* 1899. II 293.
Another compulsive image for Degas which he repeated in many late drawings and pastels. The present one is related to a pastel of 1899 (L 1340).

57 *The Bath*. Pastel, 52×35 cm., *circa* 1890. I 213, L 915.
Two drawings exist for this pastel (III 207 ii and 244) as well as a counterproof (II 372). There is also a related pastel (L 916).

58 *The Bath*. Coloured crayons and pastel on white paper, 32×47.4 cm., signed, *circa* 1892. L 1121. Musée du Louvre, Paris.
Two related pastels exist, one of which is a counterproof (L 1121 *bis* and *ter*). There is also an oil-painting (L 1120).

59 *After the Bath*. Coloured crayons on white paper, 43×33 cm., signed, *circa* 1890. Fogg Art Museum, Cambridge, Mass.
As with plate 58, a counterproof exists of this drawing (IV 360).

60 *Woman Combing her Hair*. Charcoal heightened with white, 48×63 cm., *circa* 1900. II 303.
The style of this drawing is similar to plate 54.

61 *Women Bathing under Trees*. Charcoal and pastel, 112×144 cm., *circa* 1886. IV 300, R 99, L 1070.
At the last Impressionist exhibition of 1886, two of Degas's nudes had out-door settings. This drawing belongs to a large series of nudes in a landscape, all of which were executed about 1886 (L 1070–82). There are only two later examples of nudes in landscape (L 1422–23).

62 *Two Dancers*. Charcoal, 50×39 cm., *circa* 1900. II 340, R 49.
This study of two dancers seen from the back also occurs in a drawing on tracing paper (IV 155). Degas drew the same pair of figures in the identical pose seen from the front (III 179, 265, 323, and L 1112–13), and finally produced a painting (Musée du Louvre, Paris; L 1111). He also conceived a composition with accompanying figures (III 395 and IV 263 b).

63 *Two Laundresses*. Charcoal on tracing paper, 42×57 cm., signed, *circa* 1902. R 50, V 12. A reprise in 1902 of two laundresses carrying baskets which Degas had first treated in 1876 (L 410). A counterproof exists (IV 357). Related works are L 960–61, 1418–20, and III 148 i).

64 *After the Bath*. Charcoal on tracing paper, 54.3×52.5 cm., signed, *circa* 1907. R 100, V 34. This drawing has been dated 1896–1900, but on stylistic grounds a date of *circa* 1907 seems more probable. No related pastel exists.

BIBLIOGRAPHY

This bibliography is by no means exhaustive, but concentrates on those books and articles which throw light on Degas's activity as a draughtsman.

Boggs, Jean S. *Portraits by Degas*, University of California Press, 1962
Boggs, Jean S. *Drawings by Degas*, City Art Museum of Saint Louis, 1966
Bouret, Jean. *Degas*, Thames and Hudson, London, 1965
Browse, Lillian. *Degas Dancers*, Faber and Faber, London, 1949
Cabanne, Pierre. *Edgar Degas*, Tisné, Paris, 1960
Champigneulle, Bernard. *Degas Dessins*, Editions des Deux Mondes, Paris, 1952
Cooper, Douglas. *Pastels by Degas*, Holbein-Verlag, Basel, 1952
Guérin, Marcel. *Les Lettres de Degas*, Grasset, Paris, 1945
Halévy, Daniel. *Album de Dessins de Degas*, Quatre Chemins-Editart, Paris, 1949
Jamot, Paul. *Degas*, Gazette des Beaux-Arts, Paris, 1924
Lafond, Paul. *Degas*, 2 vols, H. Floury, Paris, 1918–19
Lemoisne, Paul-André. *Degas*, Librairie Centrale des Beaux-Arts, Paris, 1912
Lemoisne, Paul-André. *Degas et son Oeuvre*, 4 vols., Paul Brame & C.M. de Hauke, Paris, 1947–49
Leymarie, Jean. *Les Dessins de Degas*, Hazan, Paris, 1948
Pečírka, Jaromír, *Drawings of Edgar Degas*, Peter Nevill, London, 1963
Pool, Phoebe. *Degas*, Spring Art Books, London, 1963
Rewald, John. *Degas Sculpture*, Thames and Hudson, London, 1957
Rivière, Henri. *Les Dessins de Degas*, Demotte, Paris, 1922–23
Rosenberg, Jakob. *Great Draughtsmen from Pisanello to Picasso*, Harvard, 1959
Rouart, Denis. *Degas à la Recherche de sa Technique*, Floury, Paris, 1945
Rouart, Denis. *The Unknown Degas and Renoir*, McGraw-Hill, 1964
Schwabe, Randolph. *Degas the Draughtsman*, The Art Trade Press, London, 1948
Vollard, Ambroise. *Degas*, G. Crès et Cie, Paris, 1924
L'Amour de l'art, vol. XII, no. 7, 1931. Special number on Degas
Burlington Magazine, vol. CV, June 1963. Special number on Degas
Connoisseur, vols 157–158, 1964–65: Four articles by Ronald Pickvance, *Degas Drawings in English Public Collections*.

PLATES

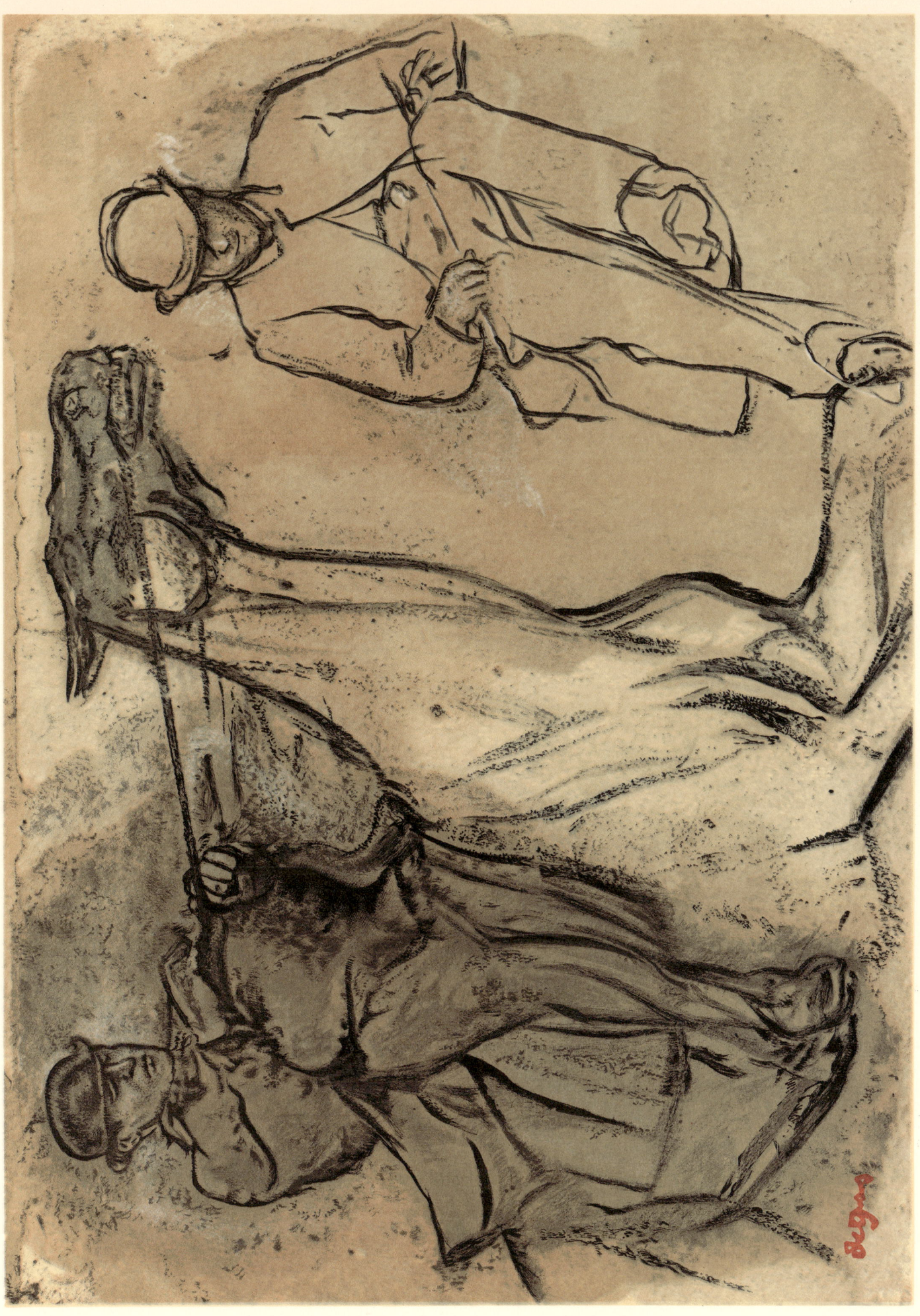

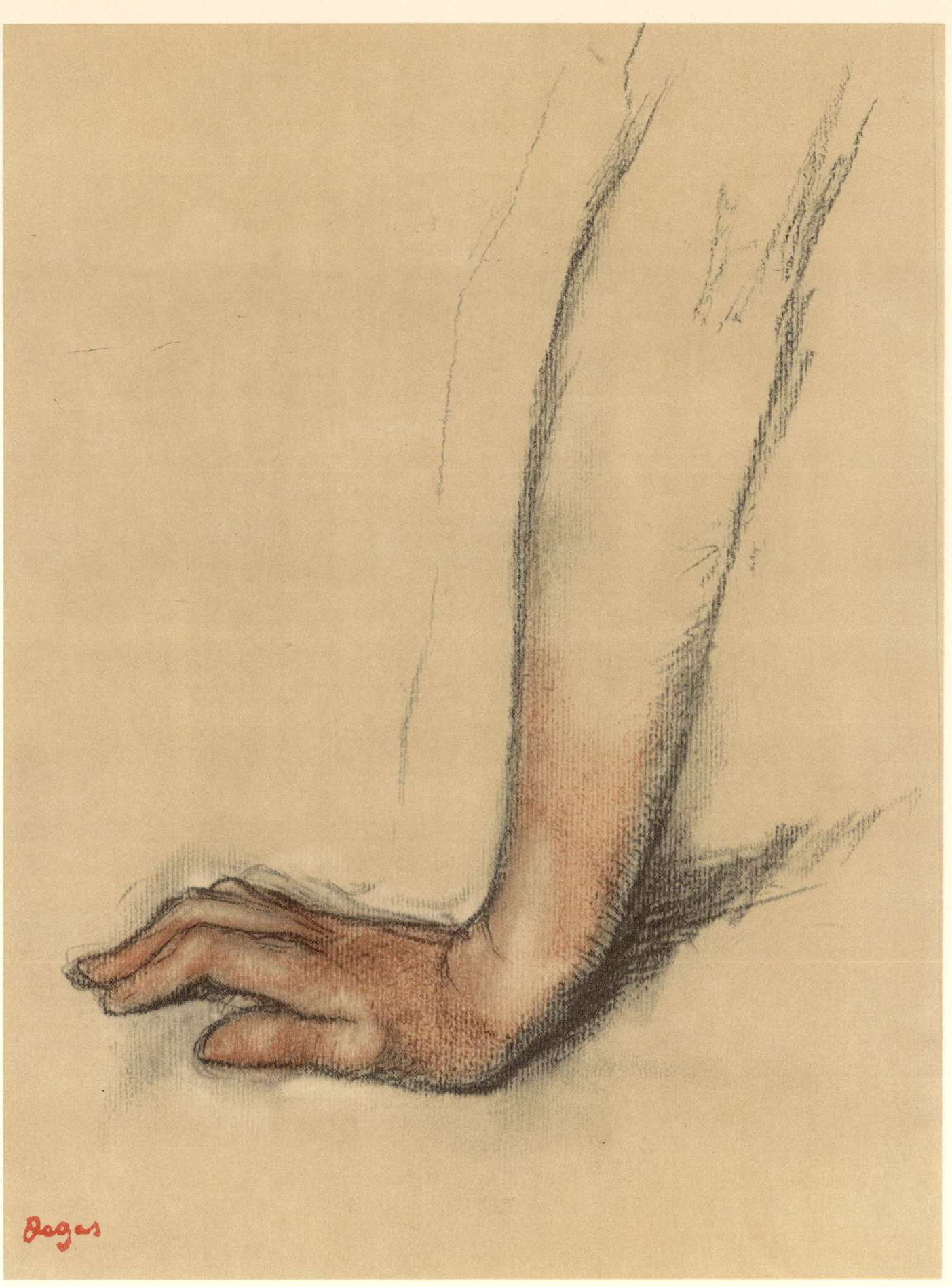

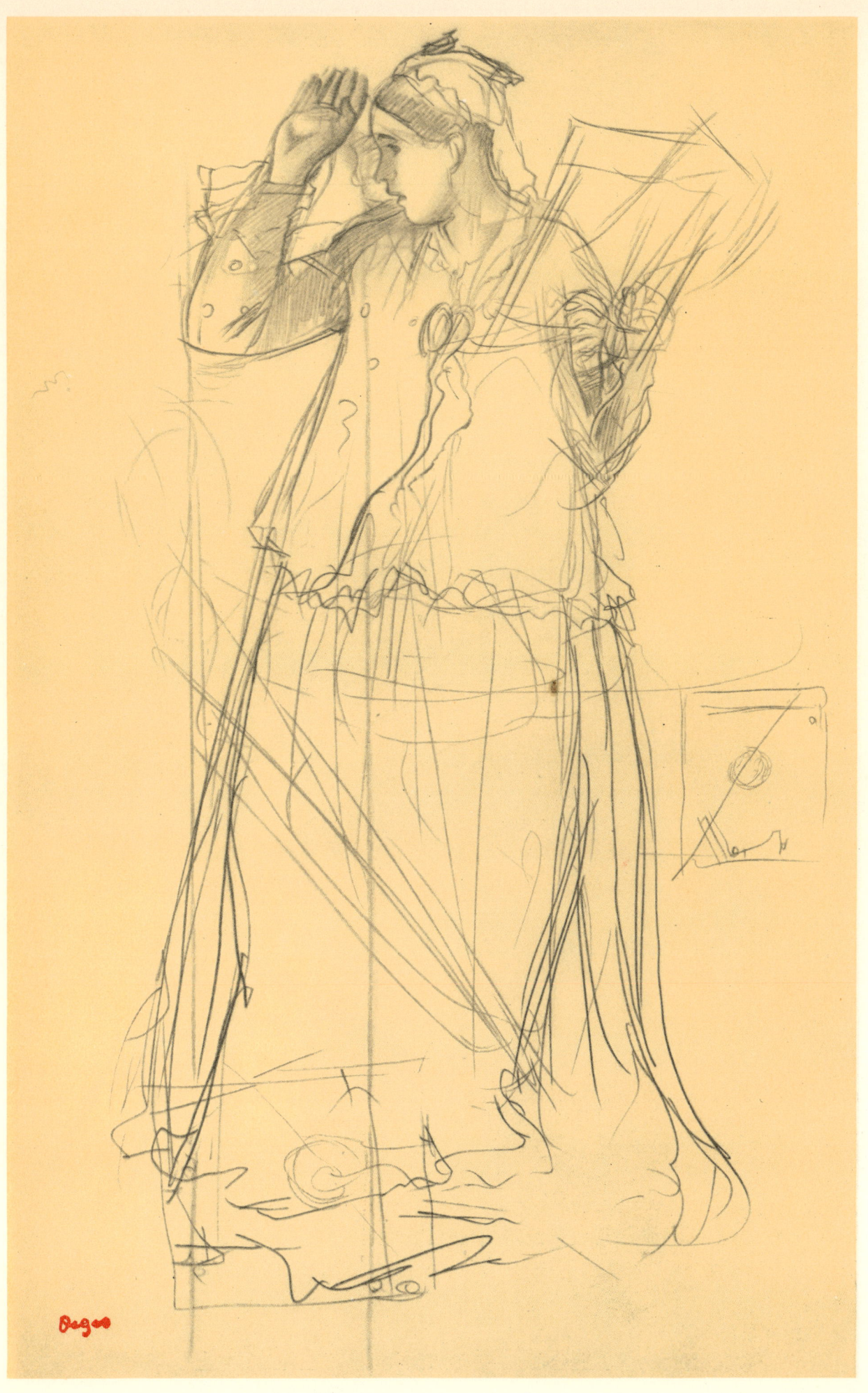

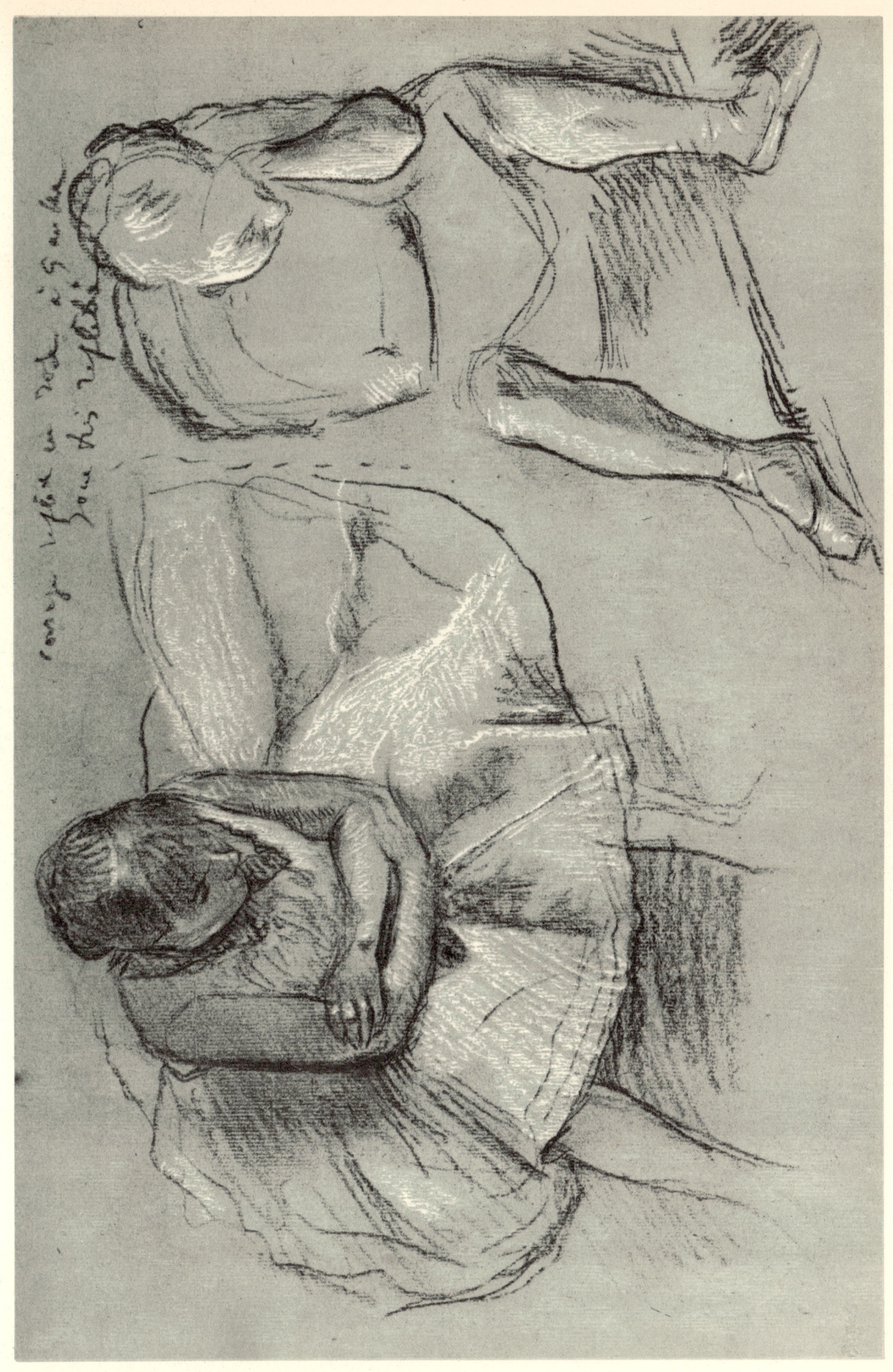

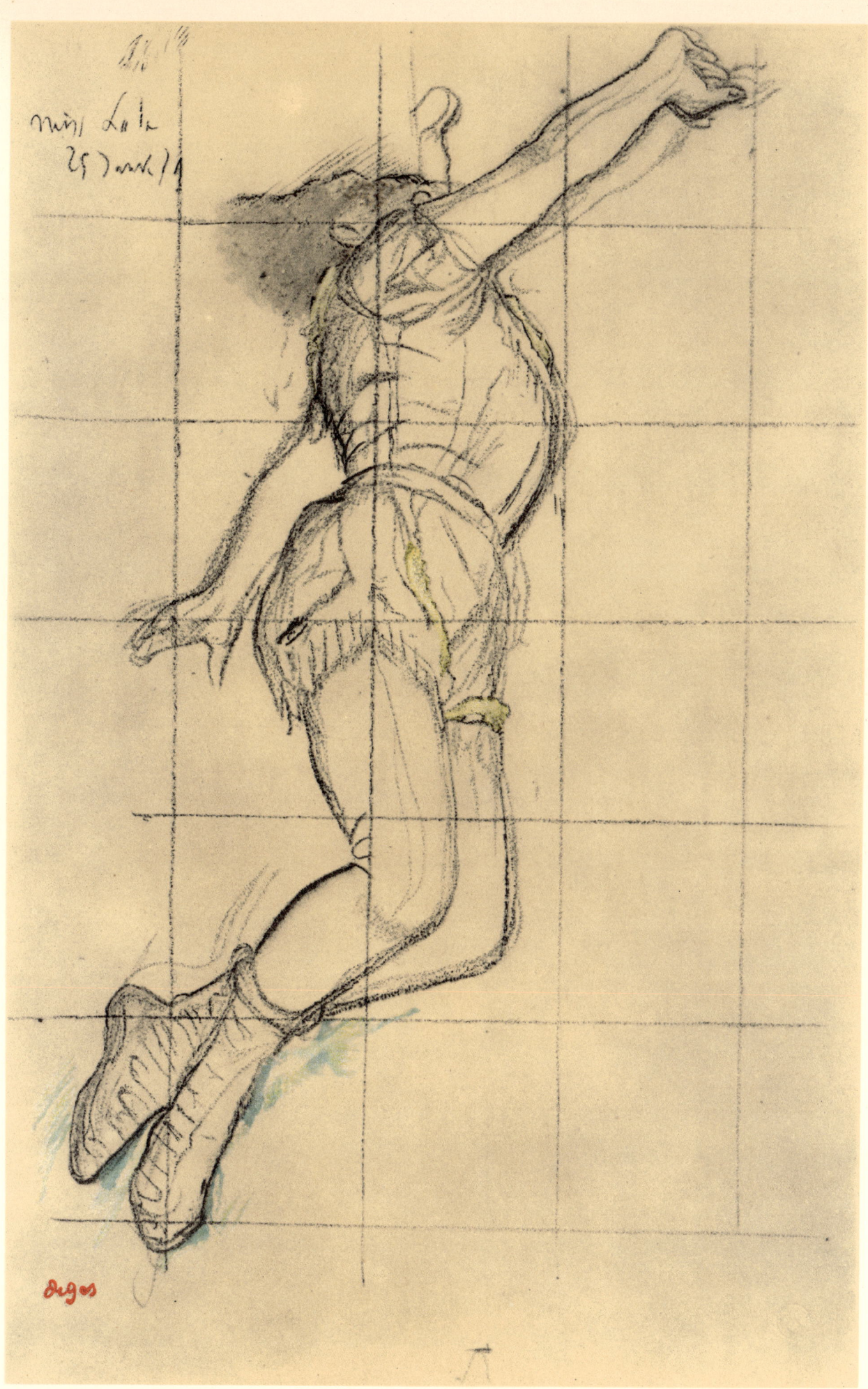

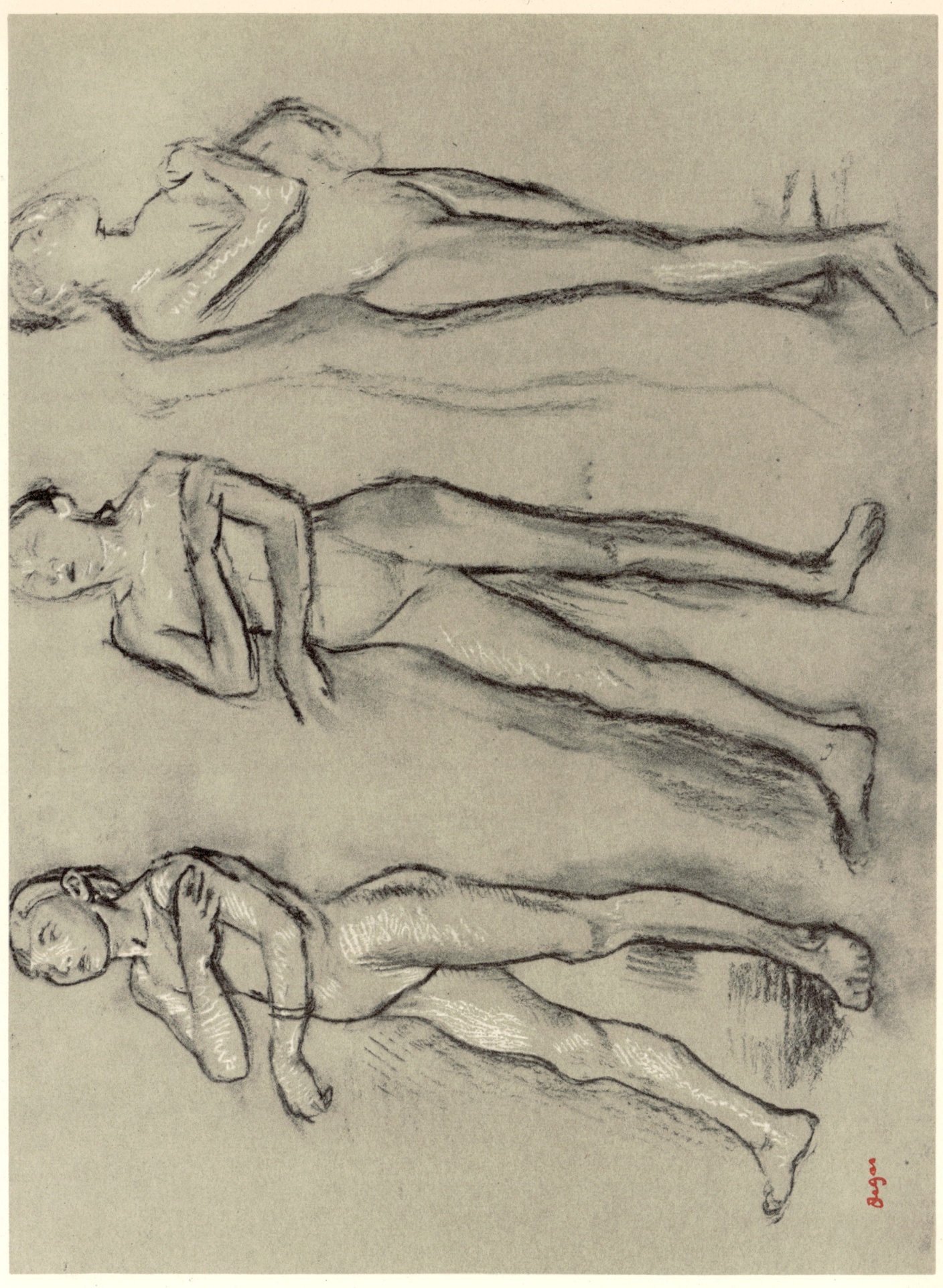

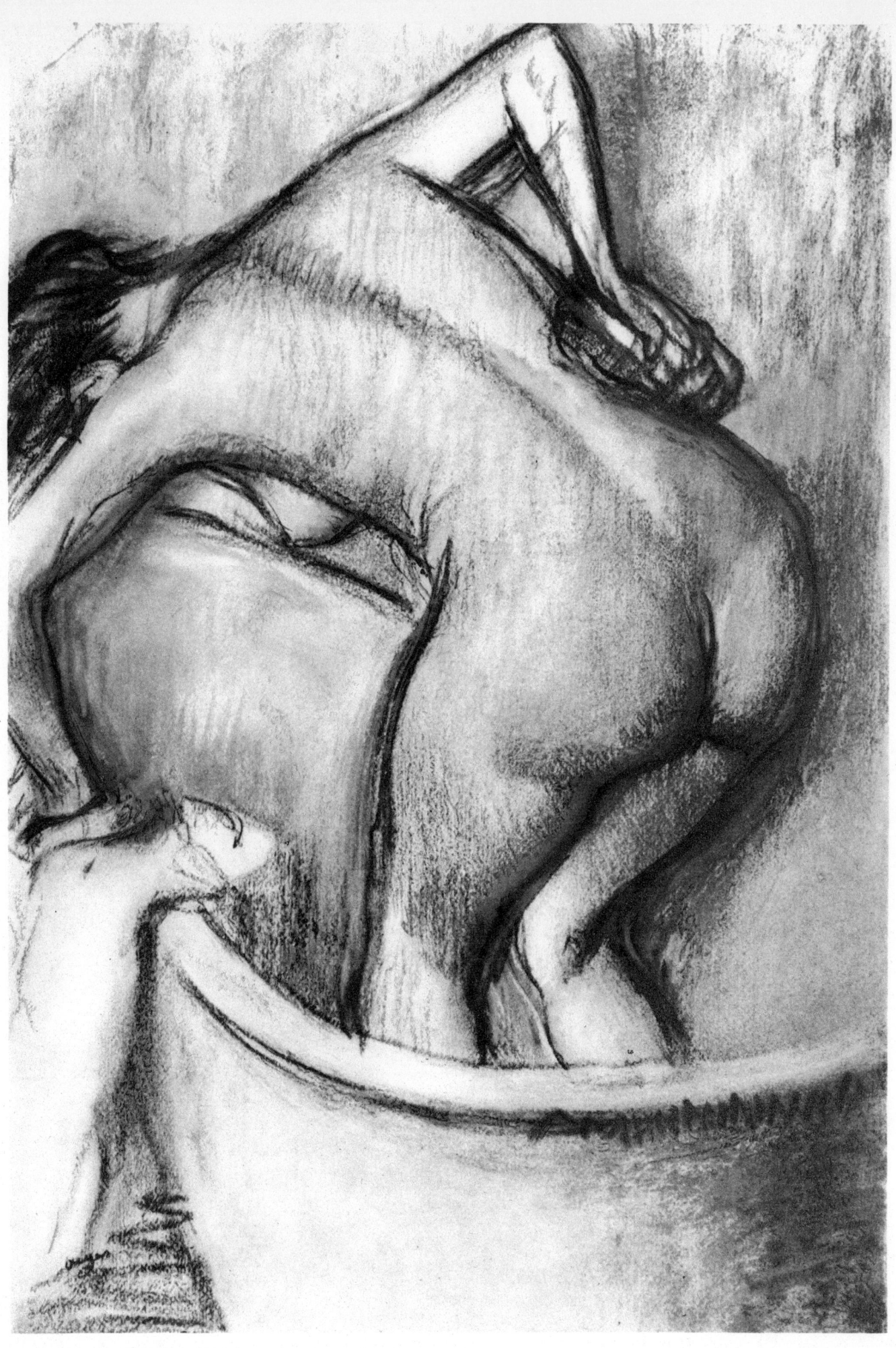

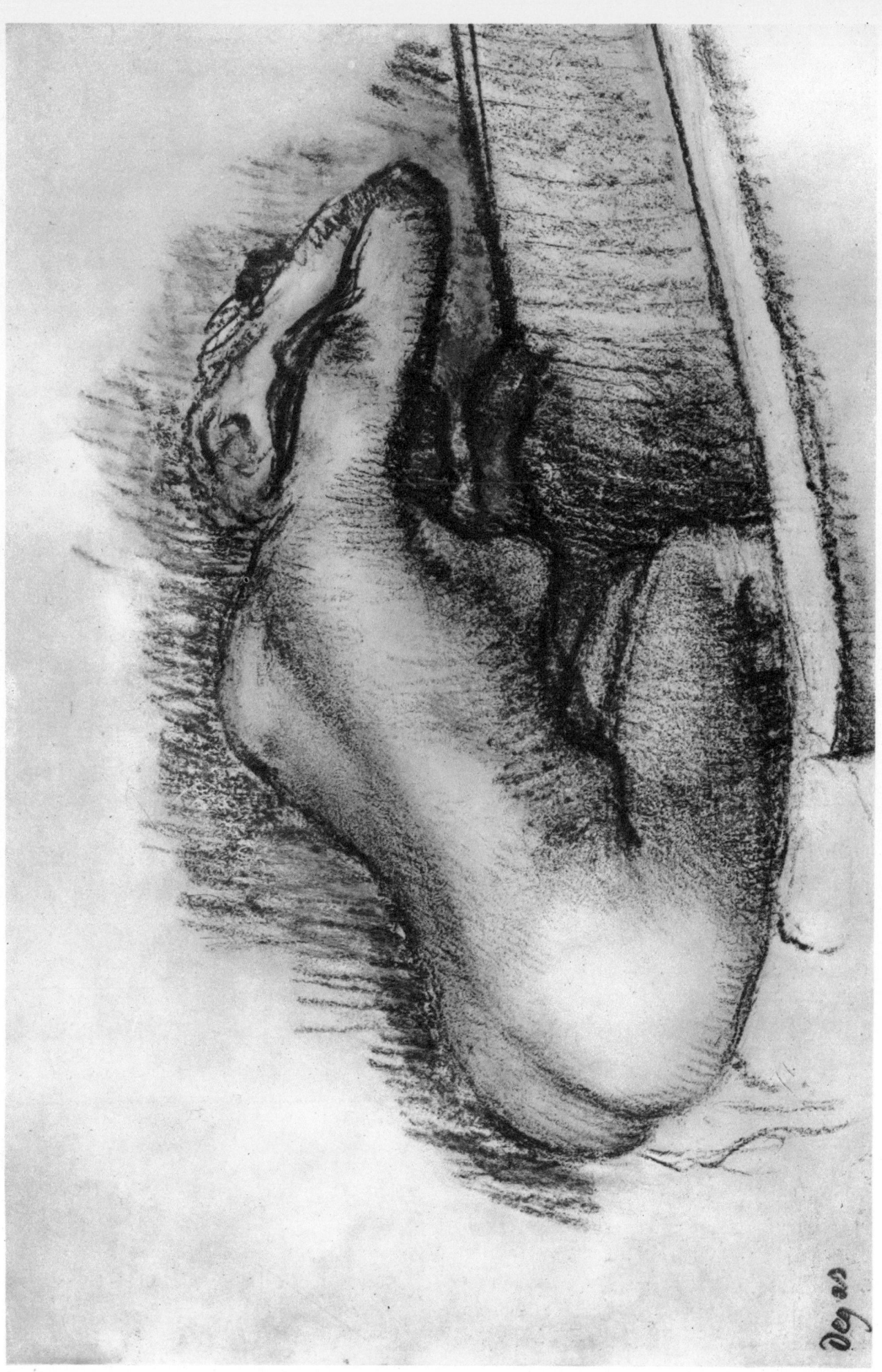